Unworldly Wise

Also by Wei Wu Wei

Unworldly Wise

As the Owl Remarked
to the Rabbit

O. O. O.

(WEI WU WEI)

Illustrations by David Eccles

SENTIENT PUBLICATIONS, LLC

First Sentient Publications edition, 2004

Cover design by Kim Johansen, Black Dog Design
Book design by Anna Bergstrom

Library of Congress Cataloging-in-Publication Data

Wei, Wu Wei.
  Unworldly wise : as the owl remarked to the rabbit / Wei
Wu Wei.-- 1st sentient publications ed.
      p. cm.
  ISBN 1-59181-019-1
  1. Taoist parables. I. Title.
BL1900.W456 2004
299.5'14432--dc22

                                                    2004000897

Printed in the United States of America

10 9 8 7 6 5 4 3 2 1

SENTIENT PUBLICATIONS
A Limited Liability Company
1113 Spruce St.
Boulder, CO 80302
www.sentientpublications.com

Dedication

Non-Objective Relation

In my absence as "me"—"you" are present as I.

Note: "You," reader of these lines, reading them are saying it also.

Deputy-Minister: But I am a profane man. I hold an office, how could I study to obtain TAO?

Shen Hui: Very well, Your Excellency, from today I will allow you to work on understanding only. Without practising, only reach understanding, then when you are deeply impregnated with your correct understanding, all the major entanglements and illusory thoughts gradually will subside.

We indicate at once that it is the understanding which is essential, without having recourse to a multitude of texts.

Shen Hui, *Entretiens du Maître Dhyana Chen-Houei du Ho-Tsö* (translated by Jacques Gernet).

"O.O.O." is a signature representing the "cube-root of zero," the algebraic sign for which, $\sqrt[3]{0}$, is not always readily comprehensible. "O," symbol of zero, represents the Subject whose objects are all numbers from one to infinity.

Contents

Preface

"Look Who is here!"

—DOUGLAS HARDING, *On Having No Head.*

ABSENT PRESENCE

HERE I am!
　　NOW I am!
　　　　THIS-I-AM!

—WEI WU WEI

Introduction

The wisdom revealed by these familiar and unfamiliar animals does not surprise me at all. Since the verbal expression attributed to them is that of their interpreter O.O.O., there is nothing unnatural or mysterious about what they are given to say. And their actions are clearly interpretations also: all is actual but not factual, like the content of our own relative "lives." Neither their lives nor ours are genuine—which is in accordance with Virtuality—but whereas our lives have no interpreter to extrapolate them for us to read about, their lives here receive extrapolation.

I have only one comment to offer: what a pity O.O.O. does not give *us* a similar treatment, and show us what is really going on in our own unobjectivized dimension! I think he might raise his eyebrows and reply by asking "What difference could you possibly expect? No such difference could be, for no 'difference'—difference being purely relative—has any Absolute existence as such whatever, never has had and never could have, for neither 'space' nor 'time' has any objective existence either, since relatively they represent precisely what, Absolutely, we ARE."

I fear that O.O.O. might reply to my suggestion or plea by again raising his eyebrows—a habit he has—and pointing out that human-beings have neither the charm, the frankness, nor the simplicity of our animal brothers, and that their discussions would be cantankerous and obscured by the mists of conceptuality. Perhaps, after all, may he not be right, perhaps we could not "do" it frankly and simply, as our animal friends *act*. However that may be, let us take advantage of the straightforwardness of these fellow sentient-beings and be content to profit by their more silent wisdom.

We are only asked to recognise ourselves in these brief, and sometimes gay, sketches, and to benefit by what they reveal. As for me, I have already done so, and can quite sincerely recommend the experience. I hope indeed that you, whoever you may be who are reading this, may benefit as thoroughly as I have.

—WEI WU WEI

1 ·- *Introductory*

"Getting dark," said the owl, settling on a branch above the rabbit. "Is this a good place to rest until dawn?"

"It is dawn," the rabbit replied, "the sun is rising: you have it the wrong way round."

"To you, perhaps; such things, indeed all 'things', are relative. Anyhow, I am the dawn."

"If you think so," replied the rabbit politely. "Yes, the place is excellent, peaceful, and the grass is delicious."

"Grass is not my affair in relativity," remarked the owl, "but I seek peace in order to BE. Any predatory phenomena about?"

"Rarely," replied the rabbit, "the odd biped, but I go to earth, and they don't eat owls."

"Very well, I will rest here," said the owl, "anyway I like rabbits."

"I am flattered," replied the rabbit, "and you are welcome."

"Juicy and tender," the owl added, "and sympathetic before dinner."

"Quite so," the rabbit assented, "a view which is unfortunately shared by others. That is why we live below our nourishment, whereas you live above yours."

"An intelligent bunny also!" commented the owl cordially. "I will stay. In any case I have dined."

"I am glad to hear it," the rabbit replied politely, "and I hope you enjoyed your dinner."

"A rat; rather tough," the owl muttered; "I will do better tomorrow. Good-night to you, and don't eat too much of that nasty grass: makes people sick."

"Good-morning," the rabbit responded, "sleep well: I will call you if anything predatory turns up."

"Thanks, good bunny," the owl answered shortly, closing his great eyes and swivelling his head, "I think you and I will be friends."

2 ᐧ *I Shine*

The rabbit, looking up, said to the owl, while ingesting several inches of grass, "I often wonder why you open your eyes when it's dark and keep them closed when it's light?"

"When I shine," replied the owl, "there is no darkness, for darkness is only absence of light, and then I observe you perpetually eating whatever the earth brings forth; when I cease to shine nothing whatever can appear."

"Then our worlds must be different?" suggested the rabbit.

"There are no worlds," snapped the owl, with a click of his beak, "other than what appears when *I shine*."

"And what appears when the sun shines?" suggested the rabbit.

"I am the sun," concluded the owl; "what you think you see is only a reflection in your split-mind."

"Is that so indeed?" replied the rabbit, twitching her nose dubiously. "Then why do you and the sun not shine at the same time?"

"I *am* 'time'," added the owl, "and all 'time' is my time. Moreover at this 'time' I am beginning to feel hungry."

"All right, all right," sighed the rabbit—as she dived hastily into her burrow.

3 ·~ Love

"Why do you eat so much grass?" asked the owl. "Grass is an emetic."
"I find it digestive," the rabbit replied, "and I love it."

"Why do you not eat snails?" continued the owl.
"Because I hate them," answered the rabbit.

"Impossible!" exclaimed the owl. "Who is there to *love* what, and what is there to be *hated* by whom? The two most fatuous words in our language!"
"Any two of us," the rabbit suggested, "you and I, for instance."

"Absurd," continued the owl, "how could we be two?"
"Why not?" inquired the rabbit.

"Because I am, and you are not," concluded the owl.
"But in space-time . . . " suggested the rabbit.

"In no time," snapped the owl, with a loud clack of his beak and an almost vertical swoop.
"Perhaps," said the rabbit, as she dived into her burrow, "but not this one!"

4 ⁓ *Within*

"I am this-I-am," said the owl, "absolutely I, devoid of any objective quality soever."

"Is that so indeed?" sniffed the rabbit, wrinkling her nose.

"*Objectively*, I am everything, and whatever appears in the mirror of my mind, which absolutely I am."

"You don't look like that at all," commented the rabbit.

"You are only looking at what you *see*," the owl answered; "you are looking from the wrong direction as usual."

"I can only see what is in front of me and, by turning round, what is behind."

"Quite so, quite so," answered the owl, "and you see nothing but what isn't there!"

"Then where are they?" asked the rabbit.

"Within, within," assured the owl. "*All is within*. You will see!" he added, clacking his beak and raising his wings majestically, poised for a swoop.

5 ⁓ *Fish*

"I am the Mind in which the world appears," the owl remarked to the rabbit.

"Is that so?" replied the rabbit, nipping off a juicy dandelion and twirling it in a corner of her mouth. "The thought had not occurred to me."

"It is," continued the owl, "and thoughts are not fish to be caught by beast or man."

"Why is that?" inquired the rabbit.

"They are not objects," affirmed the owl with a snap of his beak.

"Then what are they? Subjects?"

"Such a subject would be an object."

"Why so?"

"Because you make it so."

"Then can thoughts catch themselves?"

"Can fish?" replied the owl.

"Then who can catch them?" inquired the rabbit.

"The asker is the answer."

"As usual!"

"As always."

"And *who* is that?"

"The Mind in which the universe appears," said the owl severely.

"And *what* is that?" inquired the rabbit.

"I am," announced the owl, "even if you say it!"

6 ·~ *Here*

"My absence is what I am," said the owl, "and it has been called 'the Void.'"

"Yes?" commented the rabbit, toying with a savoury thistle.

"When I am absent the universe is present," continued the owl, "and even you would be welcome."

"How delightful!" the rabbit replied, skipping politely. "But where?"

"Here," the owl snapped conclusively, "absolutely HERE."

"And where exactly is that?"

"Where I am, which is where I was, and always have been," snapped the owl.

"Then where will I be?" the rabbit inquired anxiously.

"Here, HERE, of course! Where else could you be?"

"But where will there be room for both of us where you are?" asked the rabbit innocently.

"You will be present in my absence," the owl explained patiently.

"I do not see how that can be," replied the rabbit.

"You will, you will!" assured the owl, preparing his absence. "I will see to that."

7 ·~ *The Way It Is*

"How could I love *you?*" said the owl to the rabbit. "I am what you ARE."

"Is that so indeed?" the rabbit replied, delicately munching a dandelion.

"How could you hate *me?*" continued the owl; "you are what I AM."

"I never noticed it," observed the rabbit musingly.

"How could it be otherwise?" asked the owl. "Whatever we are—I AM."

"Since when?" inquired the rabbit. "Is it recent?"

"Since always," answered the owl, "there is no 'Time.'"

"Then where does it occur?"

"Everywhere; there is no 'Space.'"

"So we are really one?" suggested the rabbit cheerfully.

"Certainly not," snapped the owl, "there is no 'one.'"

"Then what is there?" the rabbit inquired dubiously.

"No 'thing' whatever!" the owl replied with severity.

"So what?" asked the rabbit, mystified.

"So, life!" said the owl, flapping his great wings and clacking his beak. 'As the Masters said so often, 'when I'm hungry—I eat, and when I'm weary—I sleep!'"

8 ·~ At Home

"This fashionable habit of 'living and dying' is a great nuisance!" sighed the owl, stretching his wings wearily.

"I rather enjoy it," replied the rabbit.

"You mean, I suppose, that you *think* you do."

"Then how can I not?"

"Thinking is only a notion in split-mind," said the owl. There is nothing factual about it whatever."

"But I *am* happy," insisted the rabbit.

"Nonsense, nonsense," snapped the owl, "there is no 'you' to be anything nor any 'thing' for you to be!"

"Pity," sighed the rabbit, "I have always thought that there was."

"Thought! Thought!!" deplored the owl, swivelling his head through ninety degrees. "A futile habit, universally condemned by the Sages."

"What are the Sages, then, who cannot be bothered to think, and how do they sage?"

"Those who apperceive," explained the owl shortly, "present a further dimensional extension."

"And what may that be?"

"A further direction of measurement—of vision," explained the owl.

"And how does that work?" asked the rabbit.

"Conceptualizing is thereby excluded," snapped the owl;

"split-mind is then whole."

"And what is the effect of that?" inquired the rabbit.

"They see directly, of course," the owl answered, swivelling back his head and fixing the rabbit with his luminous eyes, "and then, of course, 'they' are *absent*."

"So what?" mused the rabbit uneasily. "I mean, what is *present?*"

"Present?" asked the owl. "Why, everything, of course!"

"Everything?" queried the rabbit, skipping with surprise. "How can that be?"

"In my conceptual absence," hooted the owl, "everyone and everything is welcome HERE, where I AM,—and where they will be Absolutely at home!"

9 ·‿ *To-o-Wha-a-t*

"I sometimes wonder," said the rabbit, "why you seem to prefer the moon to the sun."

"Occupational habit," replied the owl. "When I shine directly by daylight others do what has to be done; when I shine indirectly by moonlight I look after things myself."

"Things—such as yourself?" suggested the rabbit, with a mischievous skip in the air.

"All 'things' are manifestations of what-I-am," said the owl severely, "extended in conceptual space-time in integral mind."

"Indeed," commented the rabbit, sampling a juicy clover-leaf, "how nice for them that must be!"

"Glad you find it so," replied the owl, "but in relativity, when my mind is split, there must be apparent suffering also. If positive and negative were equal they would cancel one another out, and equanimity, which is reintegration, would supervene."

"So that is why we have to suffer?" inquired the rabbit, "why unhappiness exists?"

"Neither happiness nor unhappiness exists," replied the owl; "no interdependent counterparts exist, they are conceptual estimations, which abolish one another in mutual negation."

"Then what *are* they?" inquired the rabbit.

"What are *you?*" replied the owl, "what is all sensorial perception, all cognizing, judging, discriminating?"

"Whatever is doing it, I suppose," suggested the rabbit. "Myself, for instance."

"As such you are only what is perceived," hooted the owl, "that is only an object in mind."

"Then what perceives what is perceived?" asked the rabbit. "I," answered the owl; "I, forever I."

"And to what or to whom does 'I' apply?" inquired the rabbit, her nose twitching dubiously.

"To what or to whom?" replied the owl. "Shall I tell you?"

"Yes, please do!" said the rabbit.

"Very well," said the owl, "listen and you shall hear," and—raising his wings and stretching his neck—the forest echoed and re-echoed his stentorian reply:

"To-o-wha-a-t, to-o-wh-a-t, to-o-who-o-o-om!"

15

10 ⋅ *I Who Am No Thing . . .*

"If you could say it simply," observed the rabbit, "perhaps I might understand."

"Simply what?" asked the owl.

"Simply stated in a dozen words."
"Eight would suffice," snapped the owl.

"Well, eight then—if eight is enough."
"Eight is too many, but you need them."

"As you think," sighed the rabbit; "what are they?"
"*I, who am no thing—am every thing*," said the owl.

"How can you be both when you are neither?"
"It is precisely because I am neither that I am both."

"Then what am I?"
"It is because you think you are some thing that you are not anything."

"So what?" asked the rabbit.
"So you suffer," replied the owl, deciding to dine.

11 ⋅ *The Reason Why*

"You look tired and hungry?" said the rabbit with compassion.

"I am," replied the owl.

"Then why not eat and have a sleep?"

"Nothing to eat and not sleepy."

"Allow me," suggested the rabbit, "I am available and at your disposition."
"You! Have you become a Buddhist or something?"

"Yes," shyly answered the rabbit, "it is such fun!"
"So you offer yourself to me?"

"Gladly," said the rabbit with a rapt expression, her nose twitching. "Sacrifice is great happiness."
"Sorry, not playing!"

"Why not?" asked the rabbit, hurt.
"Buddhists like that don't whet the appetite, or taste good," snapped the owl; "I prefer a rat!"

12 ·- *Doing*

"You despise us Buddhists?" the rabbit sadly demanded.
"Not particularly," the owl replied with nonchalance.

"But you told me yesterday that you'd prefer a rat!"
"Quite so, one who was prepared to sacrifice his precious 'self', if I remember?"

"Yes, this one," said the rabbit, modestly twitching her nose, "May I ask why?"
"No one to do it," explained the owl, "an absence has no flavour; digestible but not nourishing."

"I don't follow," sighed the rabbit.

"A relative presence has nothing to offer," the owl explained patiently, "and only its absence could do it."

"Why should that be?" asked the rabbit, mystified.

"What is present takes but does not give," the owl stated, "such is the nature of egoistic volition extended in space-time."

"But when it *does?*" queried the rabbit.

"Hoaxing himself," said the owl, "only Absence can DO."

"Gives me to think," the rabbit reflected timidly.

"Waste of time," the owl snapped. "Waste not, want not—just DO."

"But how DO?" asked the rabbit.

"'Do as you would be done by', and let yourself be DONE!" concluded the owl. "Anyway—you will be!"

13 ⸚ Absolutely

"I am always present," said the owl.
"How is that?" asked the rabbit.

"It is because I am always absent," explained the owl.
"I seem to remember you saying that you were only present when you were absent," remarked the rabbit quizzically.

"That also is so," replied the owl with suavity, "my relative absence is my absolute presence, and my relative presence is my absolute absence."
"Somewhat confusing," commented the rabbit; "I experience no such transformations."

"Nothing is transformed," the owl responded severely; "absolutely I am always present, relatively my apparent presence is my apparent absence as I."
"Can't you decide which you prefer?" asked the rabbit, edging towards her burrow.

"Preferences are relative and illusory," snapped the owl; "absolutely there is nothing to be either present or absent."
"Then what are you?" asked the rabbit, preparing to dive.

"Presence as such," hooted the owl, raising his great wings. "Absence as such; eternally neither present nor absent."
"Why is that?" asked the rabbit, over her shoulder.

"There is absolutely no 'where' for any 'thing' to be, nor any 'thing' to be any 'where'," cried the owl, flapping his wings ecstatically.
"And *you?*" queried the rabbit, peeping out of her hole.

"From eternity to eternity I alone AM as I. Tooo-whaaat, tooo-wheere, tooo-whooo," hooted the owl as he rose majestically, volplaning spirally in the empyrean.

"He's off!" commented the squirrel, from behind a tree.
"Relatively," added the rabbit, peeping out of her burrow, "but, Absolutely, UP."

"Absolutely, daft!" concluded the squirrel, circling his tree and leaping from a bough to the tree beyond.

14 ·- *"Après Vous . . ."*

"Whatever is seen," said the owl, "is I who am looking." "Whatever is perceived," he continued, "is I who am apperceiving." "Whatever is conceived," he concluded, "is I who am apprehending."
"What fun that must be for you!" the rabbit commented politely.

"Fun for 'you', yes," snapped the owl, "or ruddy hell—as the case may be!"
"Why for me?" inquired the rabbit, innocently.

"Because it is a 'you' who experiences it, or 'suffers' it—as the Buddha is accused of having described experiencing."
"Why must I experience, or 'suffer', what *you* see or conceive?" queried the rabbit.

"Because only a 'you' can experience pleasure or pain," said the owl patiently: "how could I experience anything whatever?"

"Whyever not?" inquired the rabbit, raising both her long ears.

"Because I, alone, AM, of course," the owl hooted; "you, other than I, are—absolutely—not at all!"

"What a pity!" the rabbit murmured, dropping one ear. "I seem to be a perfectly good rabbit!"

"Seem to be, *seem* to be!" hooted the owl, "of course you 'seem to be'; why, even those two-legged vertical monsters find you 'a perfectly good rabbit' when they cook you and put you in what they call a 'pie'!"

"And is that all I am good for?" inquired the rabbit modestly.

"All—Ab-so-lute-ly *all*," concluded the owl, "and if it were dinner-time I would give you a practical demonstration!"

"No need, no need at all," replied the rabbit hastily, "I always believe what you tell me!"

"In that case I will come down when next you feel hungry—if you will do me the honour of dining on me," the owl offered politely.

"You are too kind," said the rabbit, deeply moved, "but, well, you know, I am a strict vegetarian!"

"As you wish," replied the owl, with indifference, "as you wish. Always at your disposal phenomenally. These gestures are perfectly mutual in relativity."

15 ·- *Laissé Pour Compte*

"When the ultimate object is negated by the ultimate subject, I shall remain as I," stated the owl.

"Won't you feel rather lonely," asked the rabbit, "if such a thing should ever happen?"

"Who could there be to feel anything?" replied the owl; "there is no 'you.'"

"Then who remains?" asked the rabbit, one ear raised.

"I, of course, how could I not remain? There is no 'I' not to remain."

"Then who is it who remains?" demanded the rabbit, raising her other ear.

"I remain, of course," urged the owl patiently, "there is no 'who.'"

"Puzzling for a poor vegetarian!" commented the rabbit with humility.

"'Who's are extended in 'space' and in 'duration', vegetarian or not," explained the owl, "and there aren't any."

"Seems a pity to me," sighed the rabbit, dropping both ears dejectedly; "what would life be like without them?"

"What is life like *with* them?" suggested the owl.

"A bit of a gamble, I admit," said the rabbit, flapping both ears cynically, "but I should feel lonely."

"Impossible," explained the owl, "rodents are only spatio-temporal concepts, and 'loneliness' is relative to 'multiplicity.' As I, you could not know either."

"But as you I would no longer be me," objected the rabbit.

"Nor 'I' either, if your grammar were better," corrected the owl. "Anyhow 'me's make nonsense—there is only I."
"And 'I' *is not*—as you have often explained?"

"Precisely," the owl agreed, "an 'I' cannot be, but I am."
"Yet you are?" the rabbit objected.

"No, no!" explained the owl with inexhaustible patience. "I am, but there cannot be any such 'thing', object, as a 'you' or a 'me.'"
"So, then, you *are?*"

"Relatively. Grammatical absurdities are creating linguistic confusion!" the owl explained. "I am, and you are only as I."
"You mean that I am only as you?"

"Certainly *not*," said the owl, a trifle wearily, "I am only I, and there is no 'me', no matter who says it, or thinks he says it, acts it, does it, or lives it!"
"I almost think I understand," said the rabbit gratefully, flapping both her ears.

"You do not," hooted the owl, "as long as you 'think you understand.' 'Thinking' and 'understanding' are relative performances of split-mind in a time-context. Direct apperceiving in whole-mind, alone can reveal virtuality."
"And how am I to do that?" asked the rabbit, a trifle wearily.

"Come out of your burrow—and leave your self behind!" said the owl, with a piercing glance of his luminous eyes.

16 · ~ *Wet or Dry*

"Do I still appear to be raining?" asked the owl, opening one eye querulously and glancing skywards.

"Yes, you do!" the rabbit replied, peeping out of her burrow. "And I wish you would stop! I am hungry, and wet grass sometimes gives me a pain. Please shine, so that things may dry up."

"I shine eternally," answered the owl dryly, "it is you who conceive these distinctions."

"But you also get wet when you rain," objected the rabbit.

"Quite so," agreed the owl, "as you say."

"How is that?" asked the rabbit, mystified.

"You said 'you also get wet': as 'you', as 'a you' if you prefer, 'you' get wet—all 'you's get wet when I rain."

"Then do all 'I's shine when you shine?"

"You talk nonsense, as usual," remarked the owl; "there is no 'I' but I."

"Then is there no 'you' but you?" queried the rabbit.

"There is no 'you' at all," said the owl severely; "all 'you's are conceptual images in mind."

"Then what are we when we address one another?"

"I, always I," answered the owl, casually.

"But what is whoever we address?" queried the rabbit.

"I have told you—nothing but an image in mind: there is only I—and I am not as any 'thing.'"

"But what about me?" objected the rabbit, flapping her long ears.

"*I* am *I*," answered the owl clacking his beak, "and *you* are *I*—whoever says it; there is, absolutely, no 'me': even you speak good enough English not to say '*you* are *me*!'"

"Gives me to think," mused the rabbit, "I will meditate upon it."

"Do nothing of the kind!" too-whooted the owl, fixing the rabbit with a penetrating glance. "To 'meditate' means using split-mind: just look *from* within and see—SEE that so it IS! Stop splitting and stay WHOLE!"

17 ·– The Fact of the Matter

"When I apperceive—'you' perceive," the owl pointed out to the rabbit, "for I, alone, AM."

"Cannot I say that too?" asked the rabbit.

"When you are—you will," replied the owl enigmatically.

"Is that the essential fact?" the rabbit inquired dubiously.

"There are no facts," snapped the owl.

"Then what can one say which is true?" queried the rabbit.

"You are what I am: I am what you are," the owl stated sardonically.

"How nice for me!" commented the rabbit politely, "and for you?"

"Inevitably," snapped the owl.

"Can we all say it?" asked the rabbit.

"'Saying' is a conceptual elaboration," the owl explained; "we can all know it."

"Even dandelions?" the rabbit inquired quizzically, nipping one off.

"Why ever not?" the owl snapped. "Dandelions are sentient-beings in so far as you are! And less greedy!" he added.

"Are we not all just a little greedy?" asked the rabbit with a nervous skip.

"Differences, like preferences, are conceptual nonsense," the owl declared.

"So that even you are neither better nor worse than a

dandelion?" the rabbit asked nonchalantly.

"As 'me' no one and no thing is either better or worse than any other phenomena in mind: 'better-and-worse' is conceptual balderdash."

"How modest you are!" the rabbit commented admiringly.

"Conceptual drivel!" the owl concluded. "If you must chatter—talk sense!"

"But I eat dandelions," objected the rabbit," dandelions don't eat me!"

"And men eat you," added the owl; "do you eat men?"

"What a revolting idea!" said the rabbit, dropping the dandelion and eructating as if she were about to be sick.

"And owls eat you," the owl pointed out; "does that make you feel sick too?"

"N-n-no!" the rabbit said hastily; "that, of course, is an honour!"

"Not at all," the owl answered; "just a necessity, and sometimes a pleasure!"

"Always willing to oblige, of course?" the rabbit murmured with some hesitation.

"Quite so, as you should be," the owl responded courteously; "unfortunately hardly anybody eats owls."

"Not even rats?" inquired the rabbit.

"Don't often get the chance," the owl observed; "not very choosy manifestations either. Hardly favoured by Nature, and generally unloved, poor things; perhaps if one asked me nicely I might oblige."

18 ·– Friendship

"Well, what is it?" said the owl.

"I want to ask you something," the rabbit replied, ruminatively.

"I know," said the owl.

"I thought you would," the rabbit answered, scratching her ear with her left paw. "Why are we friends?"

"Because, of course, relatively speaking, we are aspects of one another," the owl explained.

"So that is it?" mused the rabbit. "So different—and yet mutual aspects of something!"

"Nonsense!" the owl screeched, swivelling his head and turning his great eyes towards her. "Mutual aspects of *no thing*."

"Is there really any difference?" asked the rabbit; "I mean between 'some thing' and 'no thing'?"

"Of course not," answered the owl, "If you understand that."

"Because what I am—you are, and what you are—I am?" queried the rabbit.

"Quite so," the owl remarked, "but, if you know that, why say it?"

"I know it a little," said the rabbit, humbly, "but I am never sure if I really do!"

"You necessarily know it," the owl corrected, "but you are so conditioned that you can hardly believe what you know. Why do you ask?"

"I picked a particularly luscious thistle just now, and I found myself saying 'but you are what I am'!"

"And wasn't he?"

"Yes, but it took away my appetite!"

"Conditioning! Conditioning!!" hooted the owl; "He is what you are as I, not as 'me'!"

"What is the difference?" inquired the rabbit, puzzled.

"All and none," explained the owl; "'difference' appears relatively—absolutely there cannot even be appearance."

"But relatively . . . ?"

"Relatively, for instance, your offsprings are an aspect of 'you' as 'me', as well as being what you are as I, but absolutely there can be no difference whatever."

"So I should have eaten the succulent thistle?"

"Sentiment, sentiment!" complained the owl. "If you live relatively and also sentimentally you should not eat anything, for everything by which you profit injures an aspect of what you are."

"But if I live absolutely?" asked the rabbit.

"Eat all your friends and relatives, but begin by eating yourself! Whatever difference could there be absolutely?"

"But life would be a shambles!" complained the rabbit.

"Well, what else is it, anyhow?" asked the owl, hooting and rehooting to his own echo.

"But it can be much better . . ." said the rabbit hesitantly.

"Yes, of course it can," answered the owl, "has often been, sometimes still is—just a little—and may be again at any time. But then it will be a result of direct apprehending and not of any relative method of attainment."

"Seems difficult to live like that," complained the rabbit.

"Don't live like anything," insisted the owl; "let yourself be lived: you will, you must, anyhow!"

"Even that seems difficult to me!" said the rabbit.

"Difficult? Nonsense!" said the owl. "If you *apperceive* that all things are aspects of what you are as I, they will all be what-you-are, and if you *perceive* that some things are aspects of what you are as 'me' you will regard them relatively as aspects of 'yourself', that is affectively. If other 'you's do likewise conflict will be replaced by equanimity."

"But they may dispute my personal needs?"

"If they too have understood—they will *not*," said the owl; "they will be at your disposal—as I am."

"Which is what we mean by being 'friends'?"

"Precisely," concluded the owl, "that is the answer to your question asking why we are friends."

"But will other 'me's perceive that they are aspects of what I am as 'me'?" asked the rabbit.

"I told you yesterday 'When I apperceive—'you' perceive, for I, alone, AM'," replied the owl.

"And it is I who must apperceive?" the rabbit queried.

"Only I can ever apperceive," said the owl severely.

"So that I am I?" said the rabbit, both ears aloft.

"Of course, of course," replied the owl, "what else could 'you' possibly be but I?"

19 · Loneliness

"Yes?" asked the owl.

"Thank you," the rabbit replied eagerly, "I did want to ask you a question, but I was afraid of interrupting your thoughts."

"Interrupting my . . . *what*?" cried the owl, raising his wings in indignation.

"Your, well your . . . I did say your thoughts I'm afraid," the rabbit replied apologetically.

"Only wingless human-beings waste their time with

superficial objective nonsense like that!" the owl snapped indignantly, clacking his beak. "Their minds are split from soon after childhood to the grave."

"I think I have heard you say that 'space' and 'time' are 'objective nonsense' also," said the rabbit, "and I wanted to know why that is so."

"Objectively and for the same reason, they are chemically-pure nonsense," replied the owl, "but subjectively they are what you seem to be as an objective appearance."

"Why is that?" asked the rabbit, raising an ear.

"If your appearance were not extended dimensionally in 'space', and if your appearance had no duration in 'time', you could not appear," replied the owl; "is not that obvious?"

"And you could not see me?" mused the rabbit.

"You would not be there either to be seen or to look," the owl pointed out.

"So that all phenomenal appearance is 'pure nonsense'?" the rabbit exclaimed.

"One would think that you were beginning to understand something," the owl commented with surprise.

"But if that were understood everything should become clear and there would be nothing further to discuss!" argued the rabbit thoughtfully.

"As you say," snapped the owl, "could anything be more obvious?"

"Then why don't you teach it?" the rabbit queried.

"I do not teach," hooted the owl, "I answer questions, but

the askers do not seem to pay attention to the answers."

"So that when you say it you are a 'voice crying in the wilderness'," suggested the rabbit.

"An owl hooting in the empyrean," corrected the owl.

"Must be lonely," the rabbit sympathized, "the empyrean looks empty."

"Only an object can be lonely," the owl snapped. "I am not an object."

"But when you are hooting in the empyrean, are you not an object?"

"Only to you," the owl answered, fixing her with his great eyes.

"But how is that?" asked the rabbit.

"All objects are only such to a 'you'," the owl urged. "Cannot you see that?"

"And you, not being an object, are not lonely?" the rabbit asked, scratching one ear meditatively.

"All objects are inevitably lonely," the owl pointed out, "being apparently separate; split and alone they think they are unhappy. I am never lonely."

"But why is that?"

"How could I be lonely?" hooted the owl. "I am the empyrean. How-whit -how-whit -how-whooo: I who am *everything*, I who am no 'thing'!"

20 ·- The Storm

"A bit stormy today," said the owl, digging his claws firmly into his swaying branch, "better stay indoors—since you have one."

"I am potentially underground," called the rabbit through the wind whistling among the trees, "but you are high up where you are; hang on tightly—or join me down here!"

"You seem to forget," hooted the owl severely; "I *am* the wind."

"Of course, of course; I forgot," called the rabbit apologetically, "but why *must* you do it?"

"I do not *do* it," hooted the owl, "I do not *do* anything. I just *am* it."

"Bad luck!" the rabbit screamed, "must be worse for you up there than it is for me down here!"

"It certainly is—*relatively*," replied the owl. "But, after all, why not?"

"Seems only fair to me," hazarded the rabbit, "since you *are* it."

"But you are it also, you ass!" the owl hooted back.

"I never thought of that!" the rabbit called, diving out of the way of a falling branch; "but am I a donkey too?"

"I was using the term figuratively," the owl screeched back, "but of course you are nevertheless."

"And as stupid as that also?" the rabbit queried.

"Donkeys are not stupid at all," the owl replied, "it is a

human locution—and idiotic, as usual where other animals are in question. It is as they appear in the split-mind of self-infatuated bipeds."

At that moment the branch broke off, and the owl flapped down beside the rabbit.

"Better down here," he remarked, "in an emergency at least; any rats about or other rascally rodents?"

"Not in this weather!" exclaimed the rabbit, "but may I offer you hospitality?"

"Thanks indeed," said the owl, "but I could not return it, and I should not be able to spread my wings if you asked me an unusually stupid question."

"Harmless friends are better than dangerous enemies," urged the rabbit; "you would be safer in my house."

"Safety is relative," explained the owl, shouting down the wind, "friends and enemies also. All that is my eye."

"Quite so," commented the rabbit slyly, "and lucky we have two."

"We have two of everything," the owl assented, "or of almost everything that matters. I so arranged it."

"How clever of you, and what foresight!" said the rabbit ingratiatingly. "I am so proud to have such a friend."

"My dear good bunny," said the owl affectionately, "what difference could there be between 'friends' and 'enemies'? The ones have as good a flavour as the others!"

"Yes, yes, of course," replied the rabbit nervously, "but, but if a rat were to attack me now—would you not defend me?"

"Of course, of course," the owl assured her warmly, "rats are much more savoury than rabbits!"

"Is that your definition of 'love'?" asked the rabbit, slightly offended.

"'Love', 'hate', what possible difference could there be?" asked the owl. "Neither is anything whatever except in relation to the other!"

"Then wherein does the difference lie?" asked the rabbit.

"There is no difference between opposing concepts," the owl explained patiently, removing a large twig which had fallen on the rabbit's head.

"Thanks. But wherein lies the *apparent* difference?" she inquired.

"Differences are purely conceptual, products of split-mind," he explained; "their origin could not possibly contain 'difference'!"

"Then what is their origin?" asked the rabbit.

"I am their origin," the owl assured kindly, "but allow me to offer you the protection of my wing: I am invulnerable whereas you are not, and objects are falling in all directions. All objects are potentially dangerous to those who have not apperceived that what they are is I."

21 ·- Who Dunnit?

"You are forgetting *who*-you-are, and remembering *what*-you-are-not!" said the squirrel.

"Instead of . . . ?" murmured the rabbit scratching one ear

hesitantly with her right paw.

"Instead of forgetting *what*-you-are-not, and remembering *who*-you-are."

"A bit confusing," replied the rabbit, scratching the other ear with her left paw.

"Becomes automatic," stated the squirrel, "but excuse me, here comes that owl, and he gives me the shivers; I must be off."

"Morning!" said the owl, as he settled on his bough.

"Evening!" replied the rabbit, "it is the moon you are looking at, not the sun."

"Quite so," replied the owl, "morning to me. Interdependent counterparts are personal in relativity."

"Yes, yes, of course!" agreed the rabbit apologetically.

"What are you up to?" asked the owl, after a pause.

"Nothing!" replied the rabbit innocently.

"Oh yes you are!" scolded the owl, "you're *thinking!* I've told you not to do that! What nonsense have you thought up?"

"I was only forgetting what-I-am-not, and remembering who-I-am," replied the rabbit, flourishing a dandelion with assumed nonchalance.

"Less idiotic the other way round," the owl commented, "but neither is true. Both positive, and both nonsense."

"Why is that?" asked the rabbit, disappointed.

"Everything positive is necessarily nonsense."
"But why?"

"Who is doing either?" the owl demanded.
"Well, I am!" the rabbit replied.

"If you know you are doing it, you are only trying to fool yourself!" the owl hooted. "What sort of an ass put that nonsense into your head?"

"Not a donkey, just that young squirrel who fancies himself metaphysically."

"He's nuts," said the owl, "comes from eating things like that."

"But it sounds sensible to me," objected the rabbit.

"Of course it sounds sensible," replied the owl, "that is why it is not."

"How do you mean?" asked the rabbit.

"What sounds 'sensible' is necessarily relative, and whatever is relative is necessarily untrue," the owl explained.

"But if I forget what-I-am-not and remember who-I-am, is that not what I should do?"

"There is nothing you should *do*," hooted the owl, with lightning in his great eyes; "who are 'you' to do anything?" Anything you 'do' is done by 'a you'—even if I am the doing of it. Relatively there is nothing any 'you' can do!"

"So what?" asked the rabbit crestfallen.

"Don't try to *do* anything. Anything you 'do' must inevitably be wrong," insisted the owl, "since 'a you' does it!"

"Then what must I not do?" asked the rabbit bemused.

"Don't try to *do* or *not*-to-do anything. Rest content just to BE—then that is what you ARE!" said the owl sternly.

"How do you know that? Are you God?" asked the squirrel, peeping from behind a tree.

"Certainly I am God," replied the owl; "why do you ask?"

"Because only God could know things like that!" replied the squirrel, ironically.

"*Only* God!" snorted the owl, raising his great wings in indignation. "I am not *only* God! Being God is just one of my functions, like being the Devil, and a boring one at that! Quite relative."

"Then what are you when you are not 'relative'?" the squirrel inquired, cracking a nut with calculated nonchalance.

"I am absolutely," the owl replied, severely; "it is as God that I answer petitions, or ignore them, and fulfill suchlike relative offices. Absolutely—I just AM."

22 ·– Who Indeed

"You seem to know a good deal about those two-legged monsters who cook us in pots and roast us on skewers. How is that?" asked the rabbit.

"I know everything," answered the owl with modest simplicity.

"But how do you know *that?*" queried the rabbit.

"Knowing is 'knowing' that I cannot not know," the owl replied with finality, "you also, *as I*."

"Then are they 'enlightened'?" the rabbit inquired.

"Even they are," he replied almost sadly, "but they don't know that either."

"Do they know that we are?"

"One of them at least did, an Indian sage."

"How did he know it?" asked the rabbit.

"Because he himself 'knew' it," the owl replied. "He had a friend who was a cow, called Lakshmi, and when she died he had her buried beside his mother where only the so-called 'enlightened' were buried."

"And did other people understand?"

"'Others' cannot understand," the owl explained, "only I."

"Then, if they don't understand, what do they think?"

"They think because they 'wish' to think and cannot help thinking, because they are conditioned to think, and they imagine that when a phenomenon extended in space-time suddenly becomes aware of what-it-is—it is thereby 'awake', 'enlightened', 'liberated', or whatever they like to call it."

"And it has not become aware of what-it-is?" asked the rabbit.

"No phenomenon ever has, ever does, or ever will do—in space-time!"

"Why should that be?" asked the rabbit puzzled.

"Because only what-it-is can become aware of what it is *via the phenomenon*, of course!" answered the owl, swivelling his head and focusing the rabbit with a transpiercing glance of his luminous eyes. "Can you not see that so it must necessarily be?"

"Then what is 'being enlightened'?" asked the rabbit.
"Being what-you-are, of course," replied the owl.

"But what is that?" the rabbit insisted.
"No thing whatever," the owl answered. "What could there be for you to be?"

"And who could there be to have it?" the rabbit added spontaneously. "But then what can it do?" she asked hurriedly, as though shame-faced.
"Do?" the owl answered quietly. "It can say what you have just said without *thinking* about what you were saying!"

"So that was . . . ?" the rabbit ruminated.
"It was," stated the owl, "but not, of course, the words or the speaking."

"Then what did say it?" demanded the rabbit, her ears flapping.
"I did," snapped the owl, closing his eyes and reswivelling his head with finality.

23 ·– *"Heads and Tails"*

"Mind your head!" warned the rabbit, as a branch began to break off above the owl.
"I have no head," he stated with finality.

"No?" queried the rabbit, looking up at it.

43

"What you are looking at only seems to exist in your aspect of mind," he replied, "purely phenomenal, and conceptualized."

"Then you are headless to yourself?" asked the rabbit.

"As you are—if you would only look and see," replied the owl patiently.

"So it seems: yes, indeed," agreed the rabbit. "Then how does it work?"

"It doesn't," the owl answered. "I am the absence of my head; and all that is in it!" he added conclusively.

"Does anyone know that but us?" asked the rabbit, contemplatively chewing a bean-stalk.

"A wise biped in England even has the sense to teach it," the owl told her.

"And do they believe him?" the rabbit inquired, raising one ear.

"Too heavily conditioned," the owl answered, flapping his wings, "but many have understood; it is a direct way in, and known to ancient sages, but primarily an experience."

"Then what about the rest of us—I mean apart from our heads?" asked the rabbit ruminatively.

"Looks much as usual, of course: objective appearance in mind."

"But we are then free?" the rabbit inquired with a skip.

"I have never been bound," the owl hooted definitively, folding his wings.

"And have I no tail either?" asked the rabbit mischievously.

"You have nothing," hooted the owl, swivelling his head and fixing her with his great eyes. "There is no 'you' to have any 'thing' and no 'thing' for any 'you' to have! Moreover the one you think you have is nothing to worry about anyway."

24 · Here and There

"Sad about that poor old pheasant!" sighed the rabbit, "he had such a lovely tail!"

"What happened to him that makes you sad?" asked the owl.

"Shot by one of those bipeds."
"Sad for you, or for him?"

"Sad for him, but I'm sorry too!" the rabbit explained.
"Sad for you, and silly—but neither for him."

"Why not sad for both of us?" asked the rabbit, surprised.
"What difference could there be between 'living' and 'dying'?"

"Well," said the rabbit, "'living' is being alive, so to speak, and 'dying' is—well—being dead!"

"I do not apperceive the difference," the owl declared; "a phenomenon is an image in a psyche, and psychic images are appearances, apparently both actual and factual, whether perceived in dreams, hallucinations, or in what is called 'daily living.'"

"Yes, of course, but he had such a lovely tail!" sighed the rabbit; "did you not admire him?"

"What if I did?" insisted the owl. "All 'you's are psychic images, mine also, and all that is objectivized, all that is other-than-I."

"If you say so, but I think it matters to you nevertheless!" insisted the rabbit.

"That is only sentiment in relativity," the owl hooted. "Can it matter whether such images appear to 'live' or appear to 'die'?"

"Sentimentally indeed it *can!*" the rabbit persisted.

"That is part of the living-dream," the owl stated. "Besides, and this is the point, *I* cannot die, but only what-I-am-*not*."

"Can you live, then, or only what-you-are-*not?*" asked the rabbit.

"'Living' is only psychic imagery extended 'spatially' and in 'time'," the owl patiently explained; "I can neither 'live' nor 'die.'"

"Then what *can* you do?" asked the rabbit, courageously.

"Nothing whatever," answered the owl, "nor is there anything whatever to be 'done.' I AM."

"Sounds dull to me!" the rabbit observed, dejectedly.

"That also is relative, in contrast to its opposite," the owl insisted; "absolutely, opposites and contradictions have no meaning, and therefore do not factually exist."

"Sounds even duller!" the rabbit ventured.

"Relativity cannot judge Absolute," the owl explained shortly, "for Absolute is all that relativity is when it ceases to to be relative."

"So it is not dull?" the rabbit asked.

"It is not anything; if it were it would not be absolute but relative!" the owl observed.

"Even if it's not dull, sounds a bit *lonely*," the rabbit ruminated.

"Lonely!" hooted the owl, flapping his great wings, "Tooo-whaaat-tooo-wheeere-tooo-whooo; why, we are all HERE: it is what we all ARE!"

"Then wherever is it?" asked the rabbit.

"It is where you ARE, all that you ARE, and nothing but what you ARE," stated the owl, riveting the rabbit with a glance of his penetrating eyes. "How could you 'live' or 'die' when you ARE as I?"

25 ⌐ *"The Pure in Heart"*

"Do you see who's coming?" asked the rabbit, wide-eyed. "Open your eyes!"

"Unnecessary," replied the owl, "I see just as well when they are closed."

"Well, who is it?" she asked.
"It's the unicorn," he replied nonchalantly.

"And who on Earth is he?"
"Not 'on Earth'," the owl murmured, "a religious beast."

"Trustworthy?" asked the rabbit.
"Relatively," the owl responded, "fundamentally reliable. Runs true to form, wherever encountered."

"And does he understand how things are?" she inquired dubiously.

"He does," the owl answered, "basically at least, but he is currently misunderstood."

"Will he talk sense?" she inquired.

"Does anybody?" he replied. "To you—probably not: according to what he thinks you may understand."

"Better for you to do the talking, then," the rabbit murmured modestly.

"Probably prefer to talk to you about God," the owl hazarded.

"Can't you talk about God?" asked the rabbit.

"Talk? Yes, of course," the owl replied, "but really I have nothing to say about what I am."

"And why is that?" asked the rabbit.

"Because there could not be anything to say," the owl replied with finality.

"God be with you!" said the unicorn, bowing his horn to the rabbit, "and with you!" pointing it up towards the owl.

"And with *you*," replied the rabbit politely.

"I *am* with you," acknowledged the owl.

"Ah, yes," said the unicorn, slightly taken aback, "quite so, yes indeed. God is love," he announced, "and we are His children."

"I am so glad," said the rabbit, "love is so comforting!"

"'Love' is a concept," stated the owl, "therefore 'God' must be a concept also—if He is 'love'—whereas whatever 'God' could be is necessarily inconceivable."

"That, of course, is so," agreed the unicorn, with a courteous wave of his horn.

"Moreover 'love' is only the counterpart of 'hate'," said the

owl, "and is all my eye. Please use words correctly."

"Of course, of course," said the unicorn, with good humour. "It is a convention to call it 'love.' What word would you prefer?"

"'Unicity'," said the owl, "not accurate—no word could be, in relativity—but that at least does not confuse the issue."

"Certainly," said the unicorn, "if you prefer: 'God is Unicity.'"

"I have no preferences," replied the owl, "but 'unicity' makes sense at least."

"Indeed some sacred Scripture did say, 'The only proof of his existence is Union with Him'," the unicorn agreed.

"An Upanishad, if I am not mistaken?" the owl suggested.

"No doubt, no doubt," said the unicorn, "or, as a Christian sage put it, 'God is nearer to me than I am to myself.'"

"I am indeed," the owl agreed.

"So let us pray," suggested the unicorn; "are you agreeable?"

"Yes, indeed," said the rabbit, "what could be more delightful? Could I ask for some fresh young clover, even though it is not in season?"

"Well," said the unicorn dubiously, "we could ask!"

"Prayer is not solicitation," snapped the owl, "prayer is communion!"

"Quite so, quite so," agreed the unicorn; "how right you are!"

"Pity!" sighed the rabbit, crestfallen, "then let us pray for

51

communion."

"Communion is not a 'thing' to be prayed for," the owl explained; "prayer, true prayer, IS communion."

"Yes, indeed," the unicorn agreed, "that is so. After all, the Kingdom of Heaven is within, is it not? The Lord himself said so!"

"How true, and how comforting!" the rabbit observed.

"What He meant is true," the owl remarked, "but not as it has been translated."

"Why so?" asked the rabbit.

"There is no 'without' to have a 'within'," the owl explained; "'within' is *what* the 'kingdom of Heaven' is, not *where* it is; that is all He said and all that He meant. If He spoke, it was so that we should understand and not misunderstand."

"I do not follow," faltered the rabbit.

"The Lord was not referring to your precious inside, my dear bunny," the owl explained; "He was pointing out that the Kingdom of Heaven is 'within-ness' as such!"

"Quite so, quite so," agreed the unicorn politely, "what an admirable exegetist you are, to be sure!"

"The Kingdom of Heaven sounds splendid," interjected the rabbit, "but what of the Kingdom of the Earth? Are we not, perhaps, more directly involved?"

"I seem to remember," said the owl, "people being warned not to think that I am come to send peace on the Earth, but a sword!"

"And how!" the rabbit observed, drooping her ears with

melancholy.

"But He also said 'Of myself I can do Nothing'!" the unicorn interjected.

"An improbably obvious statement," suggested the owl. "What can any phenomenon do of itself? A real bromide!"

"But it is we who have made such a mess of it all!" protested the unicorn.

"There are no 'we'," the owl pointed out dryly, "to do or not to do anything whatsoever!"

"That is so, of course," the unicorn admitted, "but the Lord also stated 'Before Abraham *was*—I AM.'"

"Evidently," the owl declared, "as a Christian sage stated, 'The word "I" denotes God's pure essence.'"

"He also said 'I am THAT-I-AM'!" added the owl, after a pause. "Have greater words ever been spoken?"

"Indeed no," said the unicorn warmly. "I think we are all agreed, are we not, that religion is the greatest thing ever?"

"It makes us all so happy!" suggested the rabbit, sighing sadly. "Should we not thank God, with a blessing?"

"'Blessed are the pure in heart—for they shall *see* God'!" quoted the unicorn, "does not that apply to us?"

"Thank you," concluded the owl, bowing formally, "so you shall, so indeed you would be doing now if your 'hearts' *were* 'pure.'"

"How can 'hearts' be impure?" the rabbit inquired, scratching one ear.

"'Heart' in basic languages," the owl replied, "usually

means what today we call 'mind.'"

"And are our minds not pure?" she continued, lowering her eyes.

"The word 'purity' means undiluted, or wholeness, and nothing else whatever," the owl explained patiently, "but you are split, and so 'impure.'"

"So that is why I cannot see God?" mused the rabbit.

"'Seeing God' is 'being God with mind which is whole',", the owl insisted, "so that 'the Whole-in-Mind shall be God, and so shall be blessed', as so perfectly stated; also the word 'whole' is the same word as 'holy'—as our friend here would probably prefer to call it."

"That is so," confirmed the unicorn; "holy it is indeed."

"Then you mean . . . ?" suggested the rabbit.

"Such is what God is," the owl hooted, raising his great wings, "and only God is WHOLE."

26 ·– Metrically

"Friendly creatures, those religious beasts; not difficult at all!" the rabbit remarked.

"Emotional, affective approach, long and difficult," explained the owl; "only the specially gifted ever get away from their imaginary 'selves' in spite of affectivity."

"Why is that so?" asked the rabbit.

"Looking for God where God is not as God-that is objectively," the owl snapped; "a positive way is interminable! "

"Which way, then, is best?" queried the rabbit.

"There is no 'best'," the owl answered, "just roundabout or direct!"

"And the most direct?" the rabbit inquired eagerly.

"Depends on conditioning," the owl replied; "only conditioning intervenes."

"Then, conditioning being suitable . . . ?" the rabbit insisted.

"The metric, presumably," the owl answered.

"And what is that?" the rabbit asked with surprise.

"I am the *inclusive* dimension," the owl hooted; "at right-angles to each and all of the others; what could be simpler or more obvious?"

"And me?" the rabbit hazarded, timidly.

"'You's are made up of my three subsidiary directions of measurement, length, breadth, and height, which constitute volume extended in space-time," replied the owl, "whereof the phenomenal universe which consists of my apperceiving."

"Is that so?" the rabbit exclaimed with a skip of surprise. "How very curious!"

"Obvious, rather than curious," the owl hooted. "What else could 'you's possibly be?"

"But from where are they measured?" murmured the rabbit.

"From Here, of course," the owl explained, "always from Here, This, and Now—from the ubiquitous Centre."

"But where is the ubiquitous Centre, and of what?" asked the rabbit.

"Everywhere," the owl explained patiently; "there is no 'where' where it is *not.*"

"How is that?" asked the rabbit, scratching an ear.

"Because, of course," continued the owl, "there is no 'where' where it could be, nor any 'thing' of which it could be the centre."

"And however is that?"

"It is because the centre of Infinity must be ubiquitous and Here, and the centre of Intemporality eternally Now. The universe has as many centres as there are sentient-beings to perceive It."

"But all that is only measurements," the rabbit objected, "which make shapes and apparent 'things'; what is in them, what activates them?"

"I am, of course," snorted the owl, "I do: what else is there to be or to do anything?"

"And where am I in relation to all that?" asked the rabbit, perplexed.

"Why ask me?" suggested the owl; "who is asking, any-how?"

"I am, of course!" exclaimed the rabbit, with mild indigna-tion.

"Quite so!" replied the owl, "as you say."

"But I said 'I am', not 'you are'," the rabbit pointed out, twirling a dandelion in her mouth.

"As I said," the owl snapped, with a clack of his beak, "I am, whoever says it."

"But why is that?" asked the rabbit, mystified.

"Because," replied the owl solemnly, "as always, in all possible circumstances, and everywhere—the Asker is the Answer!"

"In that case I . . . I am also the Answer?" the rabbit murmured, with eyes dilating and dropping her dandelion.

"As I said," repeated the owl a trifle wearily, closing his eyes and swivelling his head, "it is getting late—Good Morning!"

27 · Subjective Reintegration

"Good-afternoon!" said the rabbit politely.

"Moo," replied the cow, munching a mouthful of grass.

"Beautiful tender grass round here," added the rabbit; "hope you are enjoying it."

"Moo," agreed the cow, without looking up.

"May I ask you a question?" said the rabbit, diffidently. "I have been hoping for the opportunity for some time."

"Moo," the cow acquiesced, with indifference.

"I fear it is a somewhat personal question, but—well—are you enlightened?"

"Moo," assented the cow.

"How did it happen, if you don't mind my asking?"

"Moo," replied the cow, doubtfully, shaking her head and making her cow-bell ring.

"My friend the owl, up there, says that you cows frequently are," explained the rabbit.

"Moo," the cow answered, with undiminished indifference.

"If he were awake, we could ask him, but he sleeps at this time of day."

"I am always awake," snorted the owl; "I shut my eyes because I shine too strongly in the day-time."

"We have a visitor," announced the rabbit, "a bovine friend of mine, and your presence is needed."

"Cows are holy girls," the owl replied, "and I am always present as no thing whatever; my appearance is only what is sensorially perceived as such by whatever sentient-being is conceiving it. I am, in fact, always present as my absence."

"You hear?" the rabbit asked the cow, "he is always, in fact, awake somehow or other, and greets you warmly."

"Moo," said the cow, picking another mouthful of fresh grass, and looking up.

"She agrees that she is enlightened," the rabbit explained, "but she seems doubtful concerning how it happened, and when."

"It didn't," the owl snorted, "and there is nowhere in which it could happen."

"But why is that?" asked the rabbit, mystified.

"Only an entity could be enlightened," the owl pointed

out, "and there aren't any. Is not that your experience?" he asked the cow.

"Moo," she assented, munching happily.

"But however can that be?" the rabbit inquired.

"A famous Indian sage of our times told everybody that what they dubiously call 'realization' already exists, and that no attempt should be made to attain it—since it is not anything to be acquired."

"And did they believe him?" asked the rabbit.

"Apparently not," the owl observed, "I am told that yearly every phenomenal biped who is interested, writes, lectures, or reads about it, 'meditates' and practises goodness only knows what in order to acquire it."

"Sounds silly to me!" ventured the rabbit. "Do you not think so too?" said she to the cow.

"Moo," the cow answered, nodding her head and ringing her bell loudly.

"Only the bipeds do it," the owl pointed out. "The same Indian sage remarked that 'realization', or 'liberation' as they sometimes call it, is 'ridding yourself of the illusion that you are not free.'"

"And even that did not convince them?" the rabbit inquired.

"To be convinced is not what they want," the owl explained, "for that would deprive them of their precious 'selves.'"

"Perhaps they would have listened more readily to ancient sages?" the rabbit suggested.

"An ancient Chinese sage told them that 'never having been bound, you have no need to seek deliverance.' Could it be more simply and forcibly expressed?"

"Hardly," agreed the rabbit, thoughtfully. "Do you not agree?" she asked the cow.

"Moo," assented the cow, collecting a large mouthful of grass.

"Another Chinese sage, one of the greatest, stated that 'to awaken suddenly to the fact that your own mind is the Buddha, that there is nothing to be attained, nor a single action to be performed—such is the Supreme Way, such is really to be as a Buddha'," the owl added.

"Definite indeed!" commented the rabbit. "But what about what is called 'liberation'?"

"Identical," stated the owl, with a hoot. "Anyhow, as another of their ancient sages put it, 'Liberation' is only liberation from the idea that there is anyone to be free!"

"Then, after all, what is it they are seeking?" inquired the rabbit thoughtfully.

"You tell us, for a change, and we will consult your friend," suggested the owl amiably.

"Well," said the rabbit, burying her head between her paws, "may it not be that when a phenomenon becomes aware of what it is—it is 'awake', 'liberated', or 'enlightened'?"

"Moo," dissented the cow, shaking her bell loudly.

"Sorry if I am wrong," the rabbit murmured, downcast.

"Not bad for a bunny," the owl said kindly, "but no phenomenon ever does, or ever could!"

"Sorry!" said the rabbit, humbly. "So what?"

"What the phenomenon is non-phenomenally becomes aware of what-it-is *via the phenomenon*, explained the owl. "Ask your friend here."

"Moo!" replied the cow, nodding her head and ringing her bell repeatedly, as she turned away and gathered a large mouthful of luscious grass.

28 ·~ Diathermy

"An odd smell this evening," said the rabbit, "hot and sulphurous, what can it be?"

"Brimstone, I fancy," replied the owl, "probably the dragon."

"May be all right up there," said the rabbit, "but dangerous down here!"

"Not at all," the owl answered, "a Western superstition; dragons are most friendly beasts, as all Eastern people know. Pick a few violets! Dragons are good fellows."

"You should know," agreed the rabbit dubiously, "but it feels a bit hot to me."

"Morning!" said the owl. "Glad to see you. How goes it with you?"

"Not too bad!" the dragon replied. "Unwelcome here-abouts; people seem to be afraid of me in the West, although I always try to do them a good turn when I can."

"I know," sympathized the owl, "cold customers tend to

fight shy of—well, of cordiality."

"Can't help it," sighed the dragon, "my heart is warm, so what can I do?"

"Forbear to be expansive," advised the owl. "Keep your feelings to yourself: a Northern convention. But here you will always be welcome."

"Yes . . . welcome," added the rabbit, stifling her chokes.

"I do my best," said the dragon sadly, "but knights in armour attack me with spears as though I were an enemy!"

"Too bad! And typically stupid," sympathized the owl. "They do not even realize that by slaying 'The Devil' they are necessarily slaying 'God' also."

"How is that?" asked the rabbit, surprised.

"Interdependent concepts," the owl replied; "how could the one be anything whatever without the other? Quite meaningless."

"So what?" asked the rabbit.

"Both or neither," the owl snapped shortly. "Relative nonsense! Difficult to make chaps like that apprehend the truth."

"The poor fellows think I am the spirit of what they call 'evil'—the Devil, in fact—because I am cordial or what they call 'hot.' But I have to try," explained the dragon, "my *raison d'être.*"

"I am sure you often succeed," assured the rabbit, seizing a mouthful of thyme.

"In the East—yes," agreed the dragon, "quite a lot of people see through the nonsense of relativity."

"But are 'good' and 'evil' the same?" asked, the rabbit, sur-prised.

"In their absence, of course," the owl commented.

"Such a pleasure to find people here who understand," sighed the dragon, calcinating a wild rose-bush with his sigh.

"But what is their absence?" the rabbit inquired.

"The absence of any relative or pseudo-entity to imagine the difference," the dragon explained.

"Always their pseudo-entity," the owl interjected, "that is the everlasting obstacle which holds them in pseudo-bondage."

"And how do we rid ourselves of that?" asked the rabbit, retiring behind a log.

" 'We' do not," the owl explained; "there is no 'we' to 'rid', nor any 'ourselves' to be 'rid' of any thing."

"Then who does it?" the rabbit inquired, puzzled.

"I do," stated the owl, with finality. "Ask our friend here."

"Indeed yes, as you say, I do," agreed the dragon, extrapo-lating his "pearl," and setting fire to a cluster of dead leaves.

"But . . . but," ventured the rabbit, hopping to rearwards of the dragon, "everything we say is said by a 'we'!"

"That is the trouble," the "owl explained, through the smoke, "there always remains a 'we' who is thinking."

"How right you are, indeed!" the dragon agreed, chasing his "pearl" round the tree. "As long as there is a 'we' thinking, whatever is said must be nonsense."

"But why is that?" asked the rabbit lolloping round in the rear.

"Because thought is relative, and verity is absolute," explained the owl, shortly.

"But what is to be done?" gasped the rabbit, seizing a leaf of green sage.

"There is nothing to be 'done'," the owl answered, clacking his beak, "only a doing—which I do."

"But how can I do it?" asked the rabbit, between coughs.

"Tell her, my friend," said the owl to the dragon, "she is a good bunny, and sometimes apperceives. Your diathermy may penetrate."

"You have just said it, good bunny," the dragon told her, "'I do it': that is the doing."

"But an 'I' was asking 'How can I do it?' the rabbit objected.

"Quite so! When you perceive that there is still 'an I' behind what you are saying, you know then that 'the snake is still in the wood-pile'," the dragon pointed out.

"So what do I do?" said the rabbit, puzzled.

"Let it be burnt out!" said the dragon, simply.

"But who does that?" the rabbit asked, surprised.

"I do," said the dragon, "that is my function, my Great Function."

"And when you do that for me . . . ?" queried the rabbit.

"You do it as I," the dragon explained.

"But how is that done?" asked the rabbit, surprised.

"I am all doing," the dragon stated, "I just do it—and the objective phantasy vanishes."

"Thank you, thank you indeed," coughed the rabbit, "I will do it!" and she dived into her burrow.

"She will apperceive," the dragon announced, reorbiting his "pearl." "With your help she will apperceive what she is."

"Your visit has been most . . . enkindling," said the owl politely; "it warmed the cockles of my bunny's heart—a veritable canicular: even I feel warmer as a result of your presence."

"Don't mention it," answered the dragon. "It is a pleasure indeed to bring warmth into the lives of people in the West!" he added chasing his "pearl" into the gathering darkness like a fire-ball in the sky.

29 ·~ Immortality

"Sleeping late this evening!" said the rabbit, "the full moon is up.

"I cannot be late," replied the owl, "'time' is *that-I-am.*"

"Relatively, of course?" commented the rabbit.

"Absolutely 'time' is called 'Intemporality'," the owl explained, "and *this-I-am.*"

"So that is why you cannot be late?" the rabbit agreed. "But phenomenally . . . ?"

"Phenomenally, I am due to integrate my noumenality,"

the owl answered.

"You don't mean that you are leaving me?" the rabbit said, dropping her dandelion in dismay.

"Leaving you, bunny?" the owl hooted. "To wherever, do you think, could I go?"

"I have no idea," the rabbit replied, relieved, "but life would be sad indeed to me without you."

"Thank you, dear bunny," said the owl, "but my phenomenal dis-appearance cannot really separate 'us', you know."

"But must you dis-appear?" asked the rabbit, appalled.

"Subjected to space-time conceptually, all appearance must dis-appear," the owl reminded her.

"Yes, but not now, I hope!" the rabbit exclaimed.

"That moment of my 'time' is almost due," he said simply.

"You must dis-appear?" murmured the rabbit, aghast.

"As your 'you' that is about to happen," the owl explained, "but, as I, it cannot!"

"But how is that?" she asked scratching an ear.

"Never having appeared, how could *I* dis-appear?" he answered gently.

"But, phenomenally . . ." the rabbit hesitated.

"Nothing phenomenal can happen to this-which-I-am," the owl said dreamily, "for this-which-I-am is not, relatively."

"But, as a phenomenon . . . ?" she murmured, again.

That-which-I-am is every thing which appears and

disappears, extended in space and in time," the owl explained, "whereby I am conscious of what-I-am."

"Then *what* are you as 'I'?" asked the rabbit, puzzled.

"I have no personal *existence* as 'I'," the owl continued, "for existence is finite—and I am not."

"You are infinite as 'I' . . . ? Yes, yes," murmured the rabbit, "but yet you exist?"

"*Existence* is objective," the owl went on, "and that I cannot be."

"You are not objective as 'I' . . ." the rabbit commented meditatively.

"*Existence* is relative," the owl added, "whereas I am absolutely."

"Nor relative . . ." the rabbit mused raptly. "Then *what* is there for you to be? *Who* are you as 'I'?"

"How can there be any 'I' but I?" the owl cried, raising his great wings . . . "I who am every and no thing . . . I who cannot even be as I!" he ended ecstatically.

"Then *where* are you as 'I'?" asked the rabbit, with an enraptured expression, her ears raised.

"In the silence of the mind—I AM!" he finished with intensity, and stretching his wings he rose slowly from his bough.

The great wings smote the air, as he rose majestically above the trees, circling in wide spirals towards the full moon.

Holding her breath, the rabbit watched him, in a mixture of awe and of horror, as he rose higher and higher in the sky until he became a mere speck above her head.

Then, suddenly, the great wings folded, and a black mass shot earthwards, fell with a dull thud, and lay in a quivering bundle of feathers at her feet.

For uncounted time she remained as in a trance. Then a peal of raucous laughter rang out in the forest, and consciousness returned.

"By your leave, good rabbit," said the hyena, "my affair, not yours!"

"Render unto Caesar that which is Caesar's . . ." murmured the rabbit, and turning to the hyena, "the things which are God's are mine."

"And what may they be?" he inquired, somewhat abashed.

"If you wish to know that," she answered, with a penetrating glance which transfixed him, "you would need to know that *you are what I AM.*"

In Memoriam

(Quoted, with permission, from *Posthumous Pieces*, Chapter 79)

I am not subject to space, therefore I know no "where,"
I am not subject to time, therefore I know no "when,"
What space-time is I am, and nothing finite appertains to me.

Being nowhere I am every "where," being everywhere I am no "where,"
For I am neither any "where" nor no "where,"
Neither inside nor outside any thing or no thing,
Neither above nor below, before nor after, at either side of any or no thing.

I do not belong to that which is perceptible or knowable,
Since perceiving and knowing is what I am,
I am not *beyond* hither or thither, within or without,
Because they too are what I am.

I am not extended in space, I am not developed in duration;
All these are my manifestations, all these are conceptual images of what I am,
For it is my absence, my absolute absence, which renders concepts conceivable.

I am ubiquitous, both as absence and as presence,
Since, as I,
I am neither present nor absent.
I can never be known as an object in mind,
For I am what is knowing, and even "mind" is my object.

—Wei Wu Wei

Other Spiritual Classics by Wei Wu Wei

❧

Fingers Pointing Towards the Moon, Foreword by Ramesh S. Balsekar
The first book by Wei Wu Wei, who wrote it because "it would have helped the pilgrim who compiled it if it had been given to him."
ISBN 1-59181-010-8 • $16.95

Why Lazarus Laughed
Wei Wu Wei explicates the essential doctrine shared by the traditions of Zen Buddhism, Advaita, and Tantra, using his iconoclastic humor to drive home his points.
ISBN 1-59181-011-6 • $17.95

Ask the Awakened, Foreword by Galen Sharp
This book asserts that there are no Buddhist masters in present western society, and we must rely on the teachings of the ancient masters to understand Buddhism.
ISBN 0-9710786-4-5 • $14.95

Open Secret
In poetry, dialogs, epigrams, and essays, the author addresses our illusions concerning the mind, the self, logic, time, space, and causation, and gives his own substantial interpretation of The Heart Sutra.
ISBN 1-59181-014-0 • $15.95

The Tenth Man, Foreword by Dr. Gregory Tucker
In giving us his version of the perennial philosophy, Wei Wu Wei brings a very different perspective to the conventional notions about time, love, thought, language, and reincarnation.
ISBN 1-59181-007-8 • $15.95

Posthumous Pieces, Foreword by Wayne Liquorman
This work was not published after the author's death. Rather, these profound essays and epigrams are "tombstones, a record of living intuitions."
ISBN 1-59181-015-9 • $15.95

Sentient Publications, LLC publishes books on cultural creativity, experimental education, transformative spirituality, holistic health, new science, and ecology, approached from an integral viewpoint. Our authors are intensely interested in exploring the nature of life from fresh perspectives, addressing life's great questions, and fostering the full expression of the human potential. Sentient Publications' books arise from the spirit of inquiry and the richness of the inherent dialogue between writer and reader.

We are very interested in hearing from our readers. To direct suggestions or comments to us, or to be added to our mailing list, please contact:

SENTIENT PUBLICATIONS, LLC

1113 Spruce Street
Boulder, CO 80302
303.443.2188
contact@sentientpublications.com
www.sentientpublications.com